THE POET SLAVE

OF CUBA

A BIOGRAPHY OF
JUAN FRANCISCO MANZANO

MARGARITA ENGLE
ART BY SEAN QUALLS

HENRY HOLT AND COMPANY — NEW YORK

Henry Holt and Company, LLC
Publishers since 1866
175 Fifth Avenue
New York, New York 10010
www.henryholtchildrensbooks.com

Henry Holt® is a registered trademark of Henry Holt and Company, LLC.
Text copyright © 2006 by Margarita Engle
Illustrations copyright © 2006 by Sean Qualls
Distributed in Canada by H. B. Fenn and Company Ltd.

Library of Congress Cataloging-in-Publication Data
Engle, Margarita.
The poet slave of Cuba: a biography of Juan Francisco Manzano / Margarita Engle;
illustrations by Sean Qualls.—1st ed.
p.   cm.
ISBN-13: 978-0-8050-7706-3 / ISBN-10: 0-8050-7706-5
1. Manzano, Juan Francisco, 1797–1854—Juvenile poetry. 2. Children's poetry,
American. 3. Slaves—Juvenile poetry. 4. Poets—Juvenile poetry. 5. Cuba—Juvenile
poetry. I. Qualls, Sean. II. Title.
PS3555.N4254 P64 2006   811'.54—dc22   2005046200

First Edition—2006
Designed by Patrick Collins
Printed in the United States of America on acid-free paper. ∞

10 9 8 7 6 5 4 3 2 1

This book is dedicated to censored poets everywhere and to my hundreds of cousins in Cuba.
—M. L.

To my loving mother
—S. Q.

Te sigan los cantares
De la paz, del amor, y buen destino
Que ofrece al Bardo que sus linfas besa
Virtud, inspiración, y fortaleza.

Songs follow you
Of peace, love, and good fortune
Offered to the poet who kisses these waters
Virtue, inspiration, and strength.

FROM "A LA LUNA" ("TO THE MOON")
BY JUAN FRANCISCO MANZANO
THE POET SLAVE OF CUBA
1797–1853

THe POeT SLAVe OF CUBA

JUAN

~ ~ ~ ~ ~

My mind is a brush made of feathers
    painting pictures of words
    I remember
    all that I see
    every syllable
    each word a twin of itself
    telling two stories
    at the same time
    one of sorrow
    the other hope

I love the words
    written with my feathery mind
    in the air
    and with my sharp fingernails
    on leaves in the garden

When my owner catches
    a whiff
    of the fragrance
    of words
    engraved in the flesh
    of succulent geranium leaves
    or the perfumed petals of *alelí* flowers

then she frowns because she knows
that I dream
with my feathers
my wings

Poetry cools me, syllables calm me
I read the verses of others
the free men
and know
that I'm never alone

Poetry sets me aflame
I grow furious
dangerous, a blaze
of soul and heart, a fiery tongue
a lantern at midnight

My first owner was sweet to me
I was her pet, a new kind of poodle
my pretty mother chosen
to be her personal handmaid

My mother
María del Pilar Manzano
a slave

Together we belonged
along with countless others

human beasts of burden
to Doña Beatriz de Jústiz, La Marquesa
the proud Marchioness Jústiz de Santa Ana
noble wife of Don Juan Manzano
who shares my name
even though
he is not
my father

Don Juan rules El Molino
   his plantation
   on this island of sugar
   and many other
   sweet illusions

These were my mother's duties:
   dress La Marquesa
   undress her
   cool her skin with a palm-leaf fan
   answer questions
   never ask
   collect milk from new mothers
   in the huts
   near the fields
   slave milk, the lotion used for softening
   the skin
   of noble ladies

This my mother accomplished:
   deliver the milk
   grind eggshells and rice into powder
   for making *la cascarilla*
   a pale shell for hiding
   the darkness
   of Spaniards
   who pretend
   to be pale
   in our presence

When the noble ladies go out in public
   milk-soothed, eggshell-crusted
   masked and disguised
   we no longer look the same
   dark owner
   and dark slaves

Now my owner is ghostly
   inside her skeleton of powder
   but I, being only a poodle,
   can watch
   I am allowed
   to know
   these truths
   about shadow
   and bright

So I listen
   when the ghost-owner calls me her own baby
   she plays with me
   and even decides
   to set my true mother
   free

Free to marry Toribio de Castro
   a man also promised
   his freedom

My father is winged, like my mother
   oh, I envy them
   what will happen
   to me
   little bird
   left behind in this haunted nest?

She takes me with her wherever she goes
I become the companion of my owner, noble ghost
   no, not a companion, remember?
   a poodle, her pet
   with my curly dark hair
   and small child's brown skin
   suitable
   for the theater
   and parties

So I bark
    on command
    I learn to whine and howl
    in verse
I'm known as the smart one who never
    forgets
I can listen
    then recite
    every word

Listen, she says to her friends
and the priest
    see how little Juanito can sing
    see how I've trained him
    watch him
    perform

Back and forth
    over and over
    country home, city home, palaces, the plantation
    only six years old, she says
    but listen to his big funny
    voice

Back and forth
    over and over
    I recite strange words in several languages
    Spanish, Latin, French

while my sweet ghost-Mamá-owner
and all her friends
listen
they are forgetful
I am rememberful
I remember there is also one more mother
in my song
a bird-mother
caged
but winged

María del Pilar

My son knows all the lines
   of every play he's seen performed
   he knows the lyrics of songs
   and the rhymes
   of sonnets and ballads
   he knows the Psalms I've taught him
   the sermons he's heard at church
   the prayers of strangers
   and curses too
   all the words of a world
   observed
   for six years

Everyone applauds at the parties
   they always giggle and clap
   so delighted
   the ladies wearing satin dresses
   embroidered with jewels and pearls
   seeing them, you'd think
   we're the clay
   of earth's daylight
   while they're distant nights
   filled with stars

Why isn't he frightened,
   so young, so observant?
   Why doesn't he just play and pretend to forget
   like the rest of us do
   when we're watched?

JUAN

~ ~ ~ ~ ~

One mother can leave and be free
    but she won't
    not without me
The other one is angry with my father,
    Toribio,
    who sews and plays the harp
    my father
    who picked me up and shook me
    calling me spoiled
    like a prince

Can't he tell the difference between a prince
    and a poodle?

This is how the ghost-Mamá punishes my father:
    with silence
    her invisible
    whip
If the priest hadn't spoken to her, the silence
    might have gone on and on forever
    the silence
    I secretly
    treasured

DOÑA BEATRIZ

~ ~ ~ ~ ~

The boy is much cleaner than poodles and parrots
    or the Persian cats
        that are always shedding their fur on my pillows
        I treat him like my own
        I tell him he's the child of my old age
        I stroke his curly hair and hold him in my arms
Oh, how beautifully he behaves!
Not a rebel
    like his father, Toribio
Not a servant
    like his mother, María del Pilar
The boy is a genius
    a pleasure to behold
    a wonder to hear
I take him in my coach and he sits beside me
    calling me Mamá
    he barely knows his other mother anymore
    now I am the real one
    if only he weren't quite
    so dark

When I leave the country houses, city houses, palaces
    when I leave without him, oh, how he screams!
    Everyone laughs

he's inconsolable
how amusing, they say,
the child actually thinks he belongs to you—
in that other way
of belonging

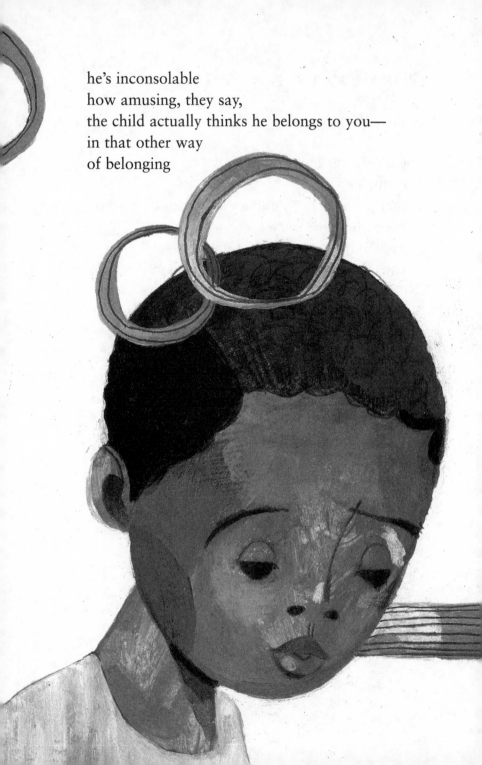

JUAN

~ ~ ~ ~ ~

What a find,
   the ladies exclaim,
   when I recite the *Iliad*, the *Odyssey*, the Catechism
   and long, dull foreign operas
   words that make no sense
   and long, boring sermons
   in Latin
   and silly plays
   that make everyone giggle
   behind the shields
   of their open silk fans

Ha, ha, a genius, isn't it entertaining
   ay, how precious
   what a find

The ghostly ladies masked and hidden
   inside their casings of eggshell-and-rice powder
   so no one can tell
   if they are dark too
   I watch
   as they arch their eyebrows
   and flutter their open silk fans

each fan the graceful shape
of a single wing
Even a free bird is helpless
with just one wing

DOÑA BEATRIZ

At his baptism I gave his mother such a wondrous,
    amazing gift
    everyone gasped
    Doña Beatriz is a saint, they said,
    not even waiting until she's
    on her deathbed
    to buy her way into heaven
    Imagine
    showing mercy so far ahead of time
    what a grand act of compassion!

The musicians were playing their harps and flutes
    the music of heaven
    his other mother's heart was drumming
    and his rebel father's eyes were roaring
    genius, I announced, the brilliant child
    of my old age

My proclamation was not trivial
    so I lifted my arms in a sweeping gesture
    my bosom grand,
    my fingers waving to show everyone
    the treasures I was free to give
    my houses were filled with such choices,

such gifts, so easily granted
all I had to do was choose one,
a painting or a marble statue
gold and silver coins
lampstands and jewels from Persia
furniture inlaid with ebony and cedar
from this island's dark, fragrant forests

I fingered the massive pendant at my neck
   diamonds, rubies, and emeralds
   all joined in a single design

Just one gift
   that was all I had to choose for a baptism
   One pearl or one coin would have been plenty
   one slim gold chain
   or carved toy

Instead, I made the announcement
   the one I had been keeping secret
   although I fear he must have guessed
   because he didn't look quite as pleased
   as I had imagined

So I wept, I dabbed my eyes with a lace kerchief
   I said the word, that one word
   they all wait for, so patiently and foolishly
   all their lives

Manumission!
I made it a big word
I waited, said it again
in its simpler forms
Freedom
Liberty
Libertad
all such fine words
so generous

My proclamation continued
in honor, I explained, of the baptism of this genius
the child of my old age
I give manumission to María del Pilar
for the price
of only three hundred pesos

And later, maybe Toribio as well
for only three hundred more pesos
and furthermore,
I hereby proclaim that from this day forward
I will abide by the Free Belly custom
of declaring all the future children
of María del Pilar and Toribio
free even long before birth, while still in the belly
hidden inside their mother
hidden, yet already free
even before she has earned and paid

her own three hundred pesos
the price of the court documents
she will someday carry
to keep the bounty hunters at bay
to keep them from seeing her and imagining
that she is a runaway headed for the mountains
ready to hide
ready to die

Ay, but my proclamation was so generous
that by the end everyone was weeping
even Juan, especially Juan
and strangely, also his mother and father
as if they imagined that three hundred pesos
could be considered
a fortune

Only Juanito, I said very clearly,
to make sure no one had misunderstood,
only this genius of my old age,
do I keep for myself
as my own
mine until the day of my death
when he will also
know mercy

MARÍA DEL PILAR

My son is not free, but I am, just as soon as . . .
    oh, but how does a prisoner like me
    find ways to earn and save such a fortune?
    How?

Imagine the shock, the excitement
    the anger, pure rage
Leave my son behind, how?
He is not hers, I won't let her have him
    why does she insist
    that he is the child of her old age?
Life is not logical, nothing makes sense
    how can this be, one child a slave
    —my child, my only child—
    while the others, unborn,
    are already proclaimed free?

I'll stay with you, Juanito, I promise
I'll always live close, in some hut of mud
    or shack of palm leaves
    your father and I, and all the rest, those still
      unborn
    your brothers and sisters of the future

we will not leave you behind
you will see us, we promise
But you must promise this
    please vow that you will not listen
    when she calls you the child of her old age
    do not listen, do not believe her, and please
    never pray
    for her death
    even though it is the only thing you will wish for
    in secret
    just as I,
    without wanting to wish such a thing
    in the presence of God,
    already find my silent self
    imagining

TORIBIO

She sends him away for a few hours each day
to the home of his godmother
to learn words

Imagine
    how he must feel in that other home
    where he learns the words
    of verses, plays, sermons, sonnets
    now he's a parrot, not a poodle
    he listens, listens, listens
    repeats every sound he hears
    from every book in his godmother's library

The applause
    when he recites at parties amazes him
    just as he amuses them with his French operas,
    a jumble of sound
    meaningless
    in my ears

They toss him gifts of coins and jewels
    silk kerchiefs

the plumes of rare birds
as if he could make wings of feathers and words
instead of playing with these toys
in his cage

JUAN

~ ~ ~ ~ ~

Three hundred pesos, is it a lot?
I like to imagine that I already have enough
   to buy them all
   mother, father, unborn brothers and sisters
   myself

Imagine
   what it would be like
   to buy yourself
   and wrap yourself up in a package
   and walk away
   carrying yourself
   under your arm
   like a book

Imagine
   how it will happen
   in just a few years
   on the day
   of her death
   doesn't she wonder
   how it feels to know that all I need now
   is a swift ending for her
   in order to make a sweet beginning for me?

MARÍA DEL PILAR

~ ~ ~ ~

I hear him, I listen, he whispers
    things other children don't know how to know
    strange words about wings and dreams,
    cages
    feathers, freedom
    death

I see him staring with those eyes
    wondering
    making me wonder
    how soon she'll die
    a frightening thought
    because if it is soon
    and if I wish or, even worse, pray
    that it will happen
    then his freedom is granted
    only as her deathbed way of imagining
    that she can buy a ticket to enter heaven
    with that one good deed
    all will be meaningless for me
    if I lose
    my own good sense
    my kindness
    my God

The other day he recited words so completely new
    that I understood the verse
    was his own
    not borrowed, memorized,
    begged from the godmother's books

Soaring
    he said
Spirit
    he whispered
Imprisoned
    he murmured
    and then he went on

I only caught a few fragments
    of his rhyme of delight,
    something about a golden beak
    something about singing
    and wishes
    and hope

TORIBIO

Now they call my son the Golden Beak
    and hearing such a flattering nickname, I ask
    myself, I ask others, I even ask God:

    Where is the rest of the bird?

JUAN

~ ~ ~ ~

Here is the house I live in
   imagine, listen, look, see
   breathe in the fragrance of blossoms
   and fruit trees
   tall and green in the roofless central courtyard
   under that tiny square of sky
   visible from deep inside
   the heart of a place
   surrounded
   by stiffly walled rooms

Mangos, orchids, jasmine, lime
   these are the scents I inhale every morning
   when I step into the courtyard
   and look up at that small square of blue
   where birds in flight pass high above
   the rhythm of rising and falling wings
   daring me
   to scratch rhymes
   by pressing the sharpness of my fingernail
   into the soft flesh
   of petals and leaves
   even though I don't know
   how to write

Would they clap for me at those parties if they knew
   about the funny shapes I invent
   like a bird's sharp little feet scratching shapes
   on moist beach sand?

Would they clap if they knew that for me
   each secret shape is seen and remembered
   as my own private alphabet
   of make-believe letters
   and words?

MARÍA DEL PILAR

Three hundred pesos
  what a long time it takes
  for a mother to earn so much money
  to buy herself free
Only on Sunday afternoons do I have the choice
  of working for coins I can save
  here they are
  just a few
so I work and work while my son does his chores
  learning trades so that someday
  when she is dead and he is free
  what a fine tailor he will become
  like his father, my own Toribio, love of my life
  sewing fragments of linen and silk
  to hold the pieces of our lives in place
  with tight, careful stitches
  seams
  buttons, hooks
like the hook-shaped fingers of the men
  who work all day in the sun in the sugar fields
  grasping each tall cane with the left hand
  then chopping it down with the right hand
  holding a huge knife, *el machete*
  the long knife I pray my husband will never be

tempted to use
in an effort to speed the slow aging of our owner
as she moves
step by step
toward her natural
death.

JUAN

~ ~ ~ ~ ~

I am the big brother of two freeborn babies, twins
  a brother and sister, my own,
  free, so free,
  while I am not.

Eleven years old and now it has happened
  there she is
  on her deathbed
  arms crossed
  eyes closed
  ghostly mask of powdered eggshells and rice
  still in place
  hiding her darkness

No matter how much I scream, shriek, weep, pray
  she will not live again
  she who called me the child
  of her old age

Don't cry, my other mother, the real one, whispers
  this is the end
  of your sadness
  now you are free!

But I'm not
it's a trick
one swift trip

to the house
of my godparents
and then to La Marquesa
instead of the long-promised
freedom.

María del Pilar

~ ~ ~ ~ ~

Five years have passed,
  and I have not been allowed
  to see my son, not even once!
We heard whispers that somehow he'd learned
  to read.
Imagine!
  No, I cannot imagine five years without my son
  and yet, it's true
  the unimaginable.

Reading? Such a scandal, his fine gift
  of genius
  along with secret tutoring
  from someone I must leave nameless
  a man who dared to teach
  after hearing him in the courtyard
  inventing verses,
  trying to scratch them
  like birds' feet on sand
  into the soft flesh
  of leaves.

Toribio

~ ~ ~ ~ ~

Tricks
    always tricks
    free, not free
    this Marquesa de Prado Ameno
    his owner
    she is vile,
    they say she's a madwoman, crazy, cruel.

I only know this much:
    she makes him wear the clothes of a page
    blue satin jacket, scarlet pants
    trim of gold braid
    diamond pin
    black velvet hat
    with two red feathers.

At least his brother and sister are free
    the twins, our freeborn children
    the girl living
    the boy dead, but free and flying
    in heaven
    winged
    no need for a hat
    with red feathers.

Juan

~ ~ ~ ~ ~

Even though I am not free
   there are things that I love
   in this world, this mansion, palace
   this strange home where I live
   even though it doesn't always feel exactly
   like living
   or home

I love to sit in the central courtyard
   looking up at a ceiling of sky
   looking around at the fragrant garden
   of jasmine and tuberose
   looking down at mosaics on the floor
   chips of tile swirled into stories
   of kings and castles
   jungles and beasts

I love the singing fountain, ripening fruit trees
   a view of high balconies dancing in wind
   the rhythm of archways and columns
   railings of wrought iron in the shapes
   of black metal peacocks
   and angels playing harps

I like to think that the angels are real
the music mine

I roam the vast rooms
    filled with paintings and statues
I dance in the ballroom when no one is looking
I try out the musical instruments
I sit in the rocking chairs, swaying
    to my own secret song
    a silent moment
    of peace

La Marquesa de Prado Ameno

~~ ~~ ~~ ~~

One more small boy-slave
   crowded onto the
   between-place
   el entresol, the mezzanine
   where he can hear me when I call
   but he cannot see me
   by looking up
   even though I can see him
   by looking down.

Here I am
   tormented
   by one more annoying
   rascal
   always reciting
   his memorized poems
   always sneaking peeks
   at my books.

Every time I catch him reading
   under a table
   or behind a door

I lock him down in the cellar
with the charcoal
to darken his thoughts
and his skin.

JUAN

~~ ~~ ~~ ~~

This is the cellar,
imagine, the fear
no floorboards, no blanket, no food
even though it's only for one day
and one night
    or maybe a little more
    just enough time to let the whip do its job
imagine, no water,
    that's the worst,
and this silence
    except for my voice trapped inside my head
    whispering verses, rhymes, curses, songs, prayers
    strange, meaningless words
and some other voice too, a comforting one,
    maybe God's
but there's the stench too, that's the devil,
    this stink of rotting garbage
    and the dampness, foul rats and ghosts,
    all the evil enchantments
the screams of another voice, a hateful one.
No. Is it true? Can it be?
How is it possible?
Is this dreadfully shrieking voice really
    my own?

I would starve
    but there are boys around my age, more or less
The boys are her sons.
Don Nicolás is the merciful one
    a whispering boy who slips me
    crumbs of sweet bread
    through a crack in the wall,
    and precious sips of water
    even though I am too weak and too stunned
    to thank him

What a strange
    unexpected answer
    to all my horrified curses
    and prayers

MARÍA DEL PILAR

~ ~ ~ ~ ~

We rarely see him anymore
    but we hear that she punishes him
    two or three times each week
There are rumors of insanity
    hers or his.

Always hungry, the whisperers say
    a child forced to hide under the table
    to find a few scraps, just like a stray dog.

If only he were a stray,
    then I could find him and feed him,
    my son.

A broken nose from the beatings.
No more golden beak.
A silenced voice.
Or so they imagine.

I know it's not true.
I can hear him singing.
That music of words.
The fluttering wings
Trapped.

TORIBIO

Some things can barely
   be imagined.

At least he has the trade I taught him.
They say his job,
   when he's not being punished,
   is sewing clothes
   of fine linen
   with trimmings.

How is it possible
   that he is no longer a child
   but a man, young and old
   at the same time?

Fifteen or sixteen, more or less
   his verses wasted
   his mind just a feather
   stitched onto someone else's
   fancy hat.

DON NICOLÁS

We let him come to our art lessons.
She lets him watch
    standing
    behind her chair

He never has a chance
    to hold a pencil
    but there is something in his eyes that tells me
    he already knows how to draw
    what he sees
    enormous murals
    filled with stories
    sketched
        in the hot, sunny
        blue air

JUAN

~ ~ ~ ~ ~

The young master Don Nicolás has given me
   a bronze pencil case
   and a stub of crayon

I listen
I watch
I learn how to draw
   eyes and ears
   eyebrows
   lips
   teeth
   a woman running
      with loose, flowing hair, weeping and running
      in a world
      made of wind

JUAN

~ ~ ~ ~ ~

Again I draw with my stub of crayon
   hiding the act of sketching
   my secret
   even Don Nicolás doesn't know
   what it's like for me
   to live in this house decorated with pictures
   on walls and doors
   ceilings and furniture
      there are paintings everywhere,
      portraits
      landscapes
      murals

Flowers
the fronds of ferns and palm trees
harps, ribbons
   birds in flight
   pleasure gardens where ladies with parasols stroll
   beside peaceful lakes

Those are the things I see
   on the walls
These are the things I draw
   for myself:

bones
the skeletons of infants
men buried with rooster feathers
and weapons
plates filled with food.

The old Africans say those are the things
buried inside these walls
under the murals of pleasure gardens
and parasols.

I am new, not old
I am Cuban, not African
I will not measure my years
by the passing of hurricanes
I do not measure the distance I travel
by counting the number of rooster songs I hear
as I pass
from one farm
to the next.

Instead of the raging, terrifying storm
I will choose to measure its silent, peaceful eye.

Instead of the crowing of roosters
I will make up my mind to count
the songs growing
inside my head.

I am new
    not old.
I am almost tired of drawing
    so many
    hidden
    bones.

La Marquesa de Prado Ameno

~ ~ ~ ~ ~

When we are at the country house, I take him fishing
   in the afternoons and cool mornings.

He baits my hook,
   sits on the roots of a wild *guásima* tree
   composing his secret verses
   imagining
   that I do not know.

Such sad rhymes, I tell him,
   even though he has not dared to recite them
   out loud.

They flicker all around him, like fireflies in the night
   stray words arranging their blinking lights
   into some sort of orderly
   rhythm.

The sight of so much invisible music
   makes me sigh.

I warn him again and again: don't make me sad
   with those flickering fireflies
   of rhyme.

DON NICOLÁS

She has him thrashed.
We have to shun him, pretending he does not exist.
She sits him in a chair in the parlor
    with signs posted all around him, warning us
    that we must never speak to him.
She hides behind the curtain
    and listens to make sure
    he doesn't cry.

He knows it will be worse if she sees him weep
    and accuses him of making her sad.
I hope he knows that when this is over
    he will fish with me again,
    and swim with me, and ride horses.
We will pretend we are brothers.

Does he ever dream of galloping away?
Once I asked.
I waited.
He did not answer.
Then I remembered: the bounty hunters.
Wanted posters for runaway slaves
    offering generous rewards.
Guns and dogs tracking men into the wilderness

into the mountains
where there are said to be
whole villages of runaways
living in caves.
Hiding.

JUAN

~ ~ ~ ~

I sit tied and gagged.
She is there, behind the curtain.
The tight cloth choking my mouth keeps me safe.
She can't hear the stories I tell myself in secret.
In silence.
Hidden.

I talk to the tables and walls.
I talk to the people and fruit trees
and horses and fish
in the paintings.

These are the stories I tell in my mind:
Fevers. Scars. Wilderness.

Once, on a day when I was not tied up and gagged,
I took some brushes that Don Nicolás had given me.
I was angry. I painted a witch.
The witch was doctoring a demon,
    healing the demon
    taking care of the demon.
    The witch was happy.
The demon was sorrowful.
Everyone who saw my painting laughed

except Toribio,
my father,
honorable tailor
a good man who wants nothing to do with magic
of the evil sort.

He took my paint brushes away.
Now I have nothing left
only verses
and secrets.

La Marquesa de Prado Ameno

~ ~ ~ ~ ~

Some people can never be satisfied.
The poet-boy, for instance.
Nothing is ever enough for him.
I have to tell the overseers to teach
    the same lessons
    over and over
    locking his ankles in the stocks
    tying him to a cross like Jesus.
Or tying him to a ladder laid out on the ground
    face down, mouth down
    so he cannot speak
    except to count his own lashes out loud.
And even then, when he loses count
    as they always do when they pass out
    from shameful weakness
Even then, when the overseer makes him start over
    counting again from number one
    until he finally reaches number nine
And even when this is done nine days in a row
    still he bleeds and weeps,
    trying to show me
    that he has won

he has triumphed once again
he has proven that he can still
make me sad.
Evil child.

María del Pilar

Sometimes he runs to us at night
    we hold him while he weeps
    ashamed to cry at his age
    a young man, not a child
    and yet, how could it be any other way
    when he is the only one in our family
    who is not free?

He is still the page at her parties
    he stands behind her chair when she plays cards
    he rides on the back of her carriage
    on the way to the country house
    or the palace of some other noblewoman
    or the theater in Havana
    where she tosses gold and jewels to the actors
    as if they were flowers, not gemstones and pearls.

He clings to the carriage
    holding a lantern all night
    many nights in a row
    until finally it happens
    he falls asleep
    the lantern drops
    he falls.

JUAN

~ ~ ~ ~ ~

Sleep enchants the human spirit.
Each time I fall into dreams
   while holding the lantern
   she sends me once again
   to the stocks
   that trap of splintered, bloodstained wood
   where ankles, neck, and wrists
   are locked in place.

I feel like an ox in its yoke
   except that pairs of oxen are free to move
   pulling the plow
   tearing down trees
   making way for more sugarcane fields
   on this island
   where once
   there were forests of cool, soothing shade
   and clearings of warm
   clear light
   and narrow pathways leading
   away.

JUAN

My mother comes from her shack
   walking on tiptoes
   until she reaches me
   hand over mouth
   to hide her shock.

Seeing me locked in the stocks
   she whispers son, *ay, mi hijo*, my son
   and it sounds like something mothers
   in many places
   far away
   must have murmured
   many times
   long ago.

Then she tells me
   Toribio is gone
   my father
   is dead.

Together we call to him
   speaking to the air
   not the ground
   not a grave.

Don Nicolás

~ ~ ~ ~ ~

I used to imagine
    that tasting dark foods
    would make me dark like him
    chocolate, molasses, or dark wild honey
    would make my mother
    whip me and lock me in the cellar.

Now I know
    that when she tells him to stand behind her chair
    while she eats or plays cards
    when she tells him to spread his elbows
    to shelter her ears
    from being bumped by clumsy serving girls
    somehow she imagines
    that his dark thoughts
    have seeped into her thoughts
    when really
    it is exactly
    the opposite.

She is the one
    with a mind
    that needs light.

La Marquesa de Prado Ameno

I let the sad poet-boy imagine
    that soon he will be free.

That way he learns
    many crafts
    preparing himself
    for the future
    as a tailor
    like his father
    or a pastry chef
    working with sugar and chocolate
    instead of ink.

JUAN

~ ~ ~ ~ ~

I let her imagine
    that I do not have
    an inkwell
    made of eggshell
    given to me
    by her own son
    along with a quill
    for writing secrets
    so that when we've heard the verses
    of some improvisational poet
    at an elegant party
    in the house of a nobleman
    I can take home the rhymes
    I remember
    and change the words to new ones
    making all words
    my own

JUAN

~ ~ ~ ~ ~

These rhymes are mine
    mine alone
    never memorized
    or copied
    in any way

Rhymes about
    soaring in spirit
    a spark imprisoned
    bursting its bonds
    of clay

Rhymes about feeling delight
    wrapped in love
    alive
    and able
    to pray

JUAN

~ ~ ~ ~ ~

Life has its moments of wonder
    and wondering.
These are the pastries
I'm learning to cook in the kitchen,
a kingdom of whispering girls:
    little spiders of ripe fried banana
    round sunsets of sliced oranges and sweet potato
    sticky mountains of coconut and caramel
    and best of all, strange creamy desserts
    from distant lands
    foreign foods with strange names like "Napoleon"
    names that make me want to read or travel
    words that make me long for a chance
    to learn

The kitchen girls whisper about crocodiles
    and water trolls
    sharks, mermaids
    caves
    forests with paths that glow
    paths of moonlight
    showing runaway slaves
    where to run

Later, when part of the sky is rainy
    and part is sunny
    the kitchen girls say that the devil
    is beating his wife
    but who would marry the devil anyway?
    No, that one must not be true.
    You have to watch out
    for other people's whisperings
    so many of them turn out to be
    tall tales
    in other words
    lies.

Juan

~ ~ ~ ~ ~

Sometimes when I am not sewing like my father
   or cooking sweets
   and listening
   to the whispered daydreams
   of kitchen girls
   I have to ride
   on the back of my owner's carriage
   all night
   many nights
   in a row
   until
   I get dizzy
   and fall
   asleep
   and fall
   with the lantern
   and fall
   landing in dreams
   landing in mud

LA MARQUESA DE PRADO AMENO

~ ~ ~ ~

He landed in the road
    the light of the lantern, my lantern
    lost
    even though the lantern itself
    somehow landed upright
    a small miracle of sorts
    pure glass, but not broken
    only one small flame
    extinguished!

He must have known what would happen
    certainly he should know how to prevent falling
    and dropping
    such a fragile glass lantern
    onto the road
    without breaking the glass
    who is he to receive such a gift
    the miracle of only one small flame
    extinguished?

Faster and faster the horses galloped
    as I shouted to the driver, run, run, run
    leave him behind
    make him walk

let him see what it feels like
to be left alone
on life's road
without light!

JUAN

~ ~ ~ ~

Imagine
  how many directions there are
  all alone
  on dark nights!

I could have walked away, to the mountains.
Even though there are bounty hunters
  with hungry dogs and pointing guns
  aren't there also caves
  for hiding?

I could have walked backward along the dark road
  instead of forward
  who says I have to follow a carriage
  when it leaves me behind?

So I stood there, alone in the darkness and silence
  imagining
  waiting to see what would happen.
He came
  the overseer
  with his whips and chains
  moving swiftly
  to catch me

before I could get away
escaping
into the mouths of hidden caves
or hungry dogs.

María del Pilar

Imagine
   how I feel
   seeing him here
   locked in this twisted
   position
   ankles and neck
   in the stocks
   my own son.
So I speak.

Silence!
   Again and again the overseer makes noise
   crying out, giving the command
   for silence

but I speak
to my son
   my own son.

The overseer is so young
   surely he will understand
   he must have a mother
   who speaks
   with love.

The first blow
   of the whip
   on the flesh
   of my son
   enters
   my heart.

Teeth and fists
   shrieking and kicking
   I punch, I attack!

Now we are here together
   both twisted
   and locked
   in our dungeon
   of sorrowful
   hopes.

JUAN

Fireflies, music, angels,
   birds, wings,
   God,
   why?
These are just a few
   of the words I find
   for songs to sing
   and rhymes to rhyme
   while my mother and I
   try to stay alive
   waiting for mercy
   or death
   whichever comes first—
   or are they
   the same?

MARÍA DEL PILAR

~ ~ ~ ~ ~

Soon your movements will be flight, he says
   the air your highway
   this is the promise he quotes for me
   borrowing hope from a verse by Arriaza
   one of his favorite Spanish poets
   pronto tus movimientos vuelo serán
   los aires tu camino . . .
   soon your movements will be flight
   the air your highway . . .

I hold this promise in my secret place
   my place for wishing and listening
   wherever that place
   may be

Soon my movements
   will be flight
   the air my highway . . .

I wait and wait
   for the movement
   of wings
   to begin!

JUAN

~ ~ ~ ~

In the darkness my mother answers my songs
    with her songs
    while we are both tied to a ladder and punished
    nine lashes of the whip
    counting out loud
    nine nights in a row
    strange novena of pain
    instead of the usual novena
    of prayers
    instead of nine rosaries prayed
    for nine nights in a row
    as if someone on earth had
    so arrogantly decided
    that God would not listen
    the first one, two, three, four, five, six, seven,
    eight times!

He listens
    I hear Him
He answers with Psalms whispered
    through the mouth of my mother
    a Psalm about the music of life
    and one about escaping like a bird
    from a hunter's trap . . .

Is it true that King David in ancient Israel
    really wrote such sad-happy doubtful-hopeful
    back-and-forth maybe-someday
    no-not-maybe
    these-are-promises absolutely-definitely
    but-we-have-to-wait
    songs?

MARÍA DEL PILAR

He keeps me alive with his whisperings
    about poets born long ago
    and poets forced to flee for their lives
    and poets catching words in flight
    like wild birds!

How can it be, this survival in chains?
How can it be, this strange vision of truth?
Just look at the overseer, look, it is true
    how can it be that I never really noticed before?
The one with the whip, he is dark
    just like us
    dark and frowning, ashamed,
    that is why he lets Juan
    give me gifts of syllables, words, songs
    old ballads about chivalry and love, my favorites
    also the one about the sailor who sings
    to calm the sea
    when the wind grows still
    fish rise to the surface
    and birds in flight pause
    to listen
    listen
    listen . . .

The Overseer

~ ~ ~ ~ ~

Strange songs, so strange they almost make me weep
    but of course I can't, I won't.
    I'm not doing anything sad.

This is life, there are people with whips
    and people with scars
    from the lashes.
    Which would you choose?
    Tell me,
    which?

Silence! I shout,
    but the noise goes on and on.
    The boy keeps whispering rhymes
    to comfort his weeping mother.
Lope de Vega, he says, naming a poet
    then whispering the verse,
    something about an angel
    telling a soul
    to come to the window
    and look out . . .

LA MARQUESA DE PRADO AMENO

~ ~ ~ ~ ~

I'm not a fool, I can tell when a rhyme is meant
    to mock me.
So when I learned that the boy
    was comforting his mother
    with lines from verses
    like the one by Garcilaso de la Vega
    about trees bending down
    so the birds
    can listen . . .

Well, just imagine
    how I felt . . .
And then there was the one by Fray Luis de León
    about the heavy cares
    of a man enslaved
    to another man's will . . .

And worst of all
    that dreadful poem
    by Andrés Fernández de Andrade
    about a nightingale
    who prefers its poor nest of feathers
    and straw
    to pleasing the ears

of some famous prince
while held prisoner
in a golden cage . . .

Well, just imagine
the boy even dares to recite the verse
by Pedro Soto de Rojas
a poem I once loved
when I was young and had dreams of my own . . .
but now . . . well . . . now . . .
it's that one, the song to a goldfinch:
You are caged
and I am caged
You sing
and I sing . . .

Hateful boy, hateful verse
how dare he make me remember
what it feels like
to want words
musical words
to yearn and sigh and wish and pray
for a song
of my own!

DON NICOLÁS

~~~~~

Someday
   when she's not paying attention
   I'll sneak him away to the city
   where he'll be
   almost free
   and we'll study
   side by side.
Someday . . .

JUAN

~ ~ ~ ~ ~

I almost feel free
    here in the kitchen
    released from the stocks
    and the whip
    and the eyes
    of the overseer
    as he stands over me,
    seeing
    my suffering

Here in the kitchen, the girls laugh and tease
    they call me silly, and giggle, and say, please
    sing to us, Golden Beak, just one more verse
    to help us dream sweet daydreams
    of peace!

So while they slice and spice and sweeten and ice
    golden pineapples made cold
    by blocks of frozen water
    brought all the way from some distant
    north
    in the hold
    of a ship
    floating,

while they do these amazing, impossible things
   I sing my rhymed daydreams
   of Kings' Day and carnivals

Just imagine, they sigh when I'm finished
how sweet to know that time passes
   the calendar moves
   like a horse
   galloping

Soon it will be Kings' Day!
We would hide piles of straw under our beds
   if we had beds like Don Nicolás and the other
   free children

Just imagine, on the morning of Kings' Day
we would find gifts
   just like the ones the Three Wise Kings
   brought to the baby Jesucristo
   in his straw-softened manger

JUAN

~ ~ ~ ~ ~

Kings' Day doesn't exist for us
    in the way it exists for them
We have to dance
    at the carnival
We're free to dance
    at the carnival!
We dance in honor
    of the Wise King, the one with dark skin
    does anyone remember his name?

We dance in the streets
    and on the plantations
    the drums are allowed on that day
    the same drums that are hidden
    all year

They let us make costumes
    that mock them
    believe it or not
    costumes so we can make fun of the
    countesses,
    dukes,
    marchionesses

Imagine!
We're even allowed to make fun of
   priests,
   nuns,
   judges,
   and armored conquistadores with uplifted
   ominous swords
We make fun of everyone, light skin or dark
   light heart or heavy
   light sky or cloudy

We make fun of ourselves
We make pain
   feel like fun

Aren't we clever?

JUAN

~ ~ ~ ~ ~

Time passes.
The rest of the calendar
    is just as strange
    as Kings' Day
    our one day of freedom
    to dance.

Holy Week begins on Palm Sunday
    seven days before Easter
Holy Week is the only week
    when women of noble blood
    cannot wear their ghostly mask,
    their pale powder of eggshells and rice
It's the week
    when they have to be humble
    so that even the dark ones
    aren't allowed
    to look light
It's the week when everyone guesses
    whose darkness came
    from the south of Spain
    from Moors as dark
    as Cuban slaves
    and which are dark because

they are
our secret
half sisters, half-slave.

Of all the strange pages
    on this island's unusual calendar
    the one that bothers me most
    comes during the bitter harvest
    of towering, sweet-flavored sugarcane
    delicious syrup encased inside stems
    as tall as a giant
    as thick as an arm
It's the season when canecutters never sleep
    when some of the priests turn their backs and
        allow
    overseers to pretend that Sunday comes
    every ten days
    instead of every seven
It's the season when weary canecutters
    with their blurred vision
    chop off their own limbs
    or drop under the wheels
    of the oxcarts
    or fall into the vats
    of boiling syrup
    or are crushed
    between the stones
    that grind the cane

and separate it from the bagasse
a fancy word
that means dry, fibrous trash
like my heart.

After the harvest, one more carnival, one more dance
one more day
of freedom to pretend
that we are free

and then the Dead Season
the time when there is no cane
to cut
and the field hands are finally
permitted
to sleep.

DON NICOLÁS

~ ~ ~ ~ ~

I would like to give mournful Juan
    a reason
    for smiling
    here it is, Juanito, my brother
    (almost)

Yes, of course I mean it, take it, this is yours
    a coin to spend as you wish
    one peseta, look, an old coin,
    no one will mind
    it's not one of those shiny new coins
    with the picture of the King of Spain
    engraved on the silver
    so you don't have to fret
    no one will think you are being disrespectful
    like the slaves who've been whipped
    or even killed
    for daring to look directly at
    colorful wild birds in the forest
    tocororo birds that wear the same stripes
    as the uniform
    of King Fernando
    don't worry, this is just a coin, not a feather,
    not a bird.

Take it, Juan, it's just a token
  a gift, let's pretend
  it's Three Kings' Day
  and you are the dark one of those
  Three Wise Kings
  what was his name?

JUAN

~ ~ ~ ~ ~

Last night the young master gave me a coin,
   one peseta
   an old coin
   not a new one bearing the likeness
   of King Fernando
   ruler and monarch of all the provinces
   and colonies of Spain
   including Cuba
   especially Cuba.

Now La Marquesa gives me one of the new coins,
   a pretty one, bright and shiny,
   with the picture of the King.
Give it to that beggar who keeps
   knocking at my door, she commands
   and almost without thinking, I switch the coins
   tossing them lightly from hand to hand
   as I walk toward the door
   open it
   place a coin
   in the palm
   of the beggar.

I do it almost without thinking,

but not completely
because really, isn't it true
that everyone is always thinking,
at least a little bit?

The shiny new coin has inscriptions
so even though its value
as money is the same as the old coin
I see a chance to read
and I take it
a chance to understand
the curls and angles
of mysterious letters,
delightful, adventurous
words.

The coin falls
the new one
intended for the beggar
who has already scurried away
thrilled to be holding my old coin.

Shameless!
La Marquesa cries out
when she sees me grabbing
the bright coin
the one that I've dropped
so now I try to hide it

but the shiny surface
and beautiful picture
and mysterious writing
make me look like I'm trying to lift a golden star
or the silver moon.

Shame!
Shouting and pulling me by the ear,
    she accuses me
    of stealing
    from beggars.

She's right,
    I've stolen,
    I've cheated
    in order to possess strange letters and words,
    letters that don't even make sense,
    so in an odd way she's right:
    I am shameless,
    shameful.
    She's always right.
    Isn't she?
    Or is she?
    Maybe we're both right.
    Is such a thing possible?

LA MARQUESA DE PRADO AMENO

~ ~ ~ ~ ~

How dare he steal my coin,
    leaving me no choice!
    He must be punished at the sugar mill
    that's it,
    I'll send him away for a few days
    or weeks
    or maybe even a few months
    what choice do I have?
    Who wouldn't do the same?

I'll have him dressed in burlap clothes
    they'll tie him to a mule
    and if,
    no, not if, but when—
    when he tries to escape:
    Hah! Just watch
    how easily they'll catch him
    and tie him again.

Just watch,
    not even my pitifully merciful,
    foolishly helpful son Nicolás
    will be able to help him this time!

Just watch,
    even my sickly husband, the Marquis,
    who rarely speaks to anyone
    and is practically invisible in this house,
    even he will try to help that boy,
    claiming Juanito the slave
    is the only one who treats him kindly
    giving him more attention
    than the Marquis gives me
    running all those errands to help the Marquis
    bringing him medicines
    trying to help,
    everyone always trying to help
    except when they should
    be helping me!

JUAN

~ ~ ~ ~ ~

Nothing to pack before leaving
   nothing to say
   nothing to watch
I close my eyes and feel the things they do to me
   instead of looking
   at the blood
   the bruises
   the pain

First there's the mule, then the boat, now the fields
   and more fields
   endless fields
   of pretty, delicious, sweet, green
   towering sugarcane
   a world of sugar
   waiting
   for the harvest

Out in the fields there are faces
   the faces of slaves
   chopping cane
   faces scratched
   by the razor-sharp leaves
faces trapped

so I keep my eyes closed
it's enough just feeling
their pain

Now I'm shackled, chained, trapped
   twenty-five lashes of the whip
   in the morning
   my breakfast of screams
   twenty-five more lashes at noon
   instead of lunch
   I taste my tears
   I eat shame

Nine days in a row
   the overseer almost apologizes
   her instructions, he says, I have no choice
   and anyway, nine is a good number
   women who pray *la novena*
   pray for nine days in a row
   just like this
   only your prayers aren't words
   just those moans

He sighs with compassion, the overseer
   saying there's no choice, he works hard
   he has to please La Marquesa
   even though nine days of whipping and moaning
   it's too much

too much for both of us
my pain, my fears
and his guilt, the screams and moans reaching
his ears

Merciful.
It's a word
 I truly understand now
 compassion
 kindness

Secretly, the overseer stops whipping
 and listening to my moans
 long before number nine
 is it possible that he can't count?

At the moment it doesn't really matter to me
 whether the mercy,
 compassion,
 and kindness of the overseer
 are his own idea
 or something that came from an angel of God
 maybe the angel
 placed a vision in the overseer's mind
 a winged picture
 of what it would feel like
 if his eyes were closed

nine days in a row
and I was the one with the whip,
watching and listening
while he moaned . . .

JUAN

~ ~ ~ ~ ~

When it's over I struggle to work hard
    trying to please
    the angel of God who sends visions of mercy,
    and trying to please this strange man too
    this watching, listening overseer
    who chose or was chosen
    to leave me
    alive

Nine days, it would have been too much
    I would have shriveled down to nothing
    just a dry wisp
    of my living self
    smaller than those tiny letters engraved
    on a coin
    above the crown
    of the King
    of Spain
    and all her colonies
    especially this island, bittersweet island
    of sugar
    and dreams

MARÍA DEL PILAR

~ ~ ~ ~ ~

Every time I manage to find poor Juan
   working and working
   out in the fields
   he tells me
   how La Marquesa always promises
   to kill him

So I answer
   with one small truth
   and while I'm speaking
   I can feel the small truth growing
   bigger and bigger
   inside my mouth
   God is good
   and good is always more powerful
   than evil
   I don't know why the devil
   even bothers
   to fight

JUAN

~ ~ ~ ~

When I'm not in the fields
   and I need to forget
   I can fold shapes of paper
   and paint them
   I can make frames of wild cane
   I can cut out the pictures of people
   from playing cards
   paper dolls
   I give them to children

I figure out how to make shadow puppets
   for slave children
   who love to see how
   lifeless puppets of wood
   learn to dance

Then I'm back indoors again,
   trapped in the fearfully lifeless house
   that will never learn how
   to dance like a home

I fight duels with poets, famous ones who visit
   there's a poet who can wiggle his ears

and one who challenges me to finish his verses
after he leaves the words soaring
like birds in midair

You've won, they tell me,
Poeta-Esclavo, you've won
and it feels good,
how they've turned the words *poet* and *slave*
into a name, first name and last name so that
when a man is my friend
he only uses the first part
calling me Poet
not Slave

Don Nicolás

~ ~ ~ ~

Ay, *no*, not again, *ay no*,
   look, *mira*, he's done it again
   Poet, how could you?
   look what you've done
just imagine
   the risk
just imagine
   what she is capable of doing to your body
   your mind and your soul
just imagine the heart or the non-heart
   of my own mother
   a sad, dancing puppet-woman
think what she will do
   when she sees how your thumbnail
   has carved shapes that look
   like whole letters, whole words
   into the succulent skin
   of this geranium leaf
   releasing
   the fragrance
   of verse

Juan

~ ~ ~ ~ ~

This time it's worse than before
   even though I never imagined such a thing
   could be possible
   pain worse than death
   here I am,
   still alive
   but sharing this locked room
   with the dead

She made them lock me inside this dark place
   all alone
   with no one but these cadavers
   for company
   dead bodies everywhere
   cold and naked, all of us,
   in a land of heat
   where we should be outdoors
   covered with green growing blankets of leaves
   in this land of flowers and birds
   paradise
   except for the shackles
   and eyes

so many eyes
eyes of the dead
staring
   staring
     staring

Do they know?
   Do they hate me?
   Can they see
   that I am
   still alive
   just barely?

Bodies seem to rise all around me
   roaming the room
   back and forth

So I stand
   afraid to lie down
   close my eyes
   rest

A broken shutter bangs
   I hear water
   a river
   a ditch
   a torrent falling over a cliff

Each time the shutter opens
    I imagine that one more spirit
    has entered
    this room
Each time it slams shut I know that I am trapped
    just one more visible example
    of death

THE OVERSEER

I turn the key in the lock.
I enter the room in this abandoned infirmary,
    hideous hospital where fifty beds
    meant for the living
    are used by the dead.

Who killed them? Why so many?
    Is it the whippings I give them?
    No, please, God, no, anything but that!

I have a timid assistant who follows me in,
    and an administrator too.
    Look at us: we are officials, we are safe,
    and yet
    there's this smell, and the silence,
    the absence of breath.
We cover our mouths with clean linen handkerchiefs,
    our initials embroidered in the corners, so elegant.
We speak through the cloth, we tie his hands,
    just like the hands
    of our Lord Jesucristo on
    the cross.

Suddenly I wonder,
  what does it mean
  to be saved
  from someone
  like me?

Then we lift him.
  We place his feet in two holes in a board;
  we tie them together, now he's even
  more trapped than before.

Before we leave him, I see blood and the mercy
  of unconsciousness.
  He seems to sleep;
  the sight of his peacefulness
  makes me pray
  that he will not enter
  my dreams
  tonight
  along with all these others,
  the dead,
  his companions.

MARÍA DEL PILAR

My wounded son is in my arms,
   in the chapel,
   weeping

I weep too
Who would not?

Even the overseer weeps
   but only for
   his own soul

And the priest
   has also shed a few tears
   of confusion
   now he tells me to leave

What choice do I have?
   I obey

La Marquesa de Prado Ameno

~ ~ ~ ~ ~

In the morning I ask if he has been treated well
　　and the administrator takes me to see him
　　in the chapel.

What a sight!
　　I smile and ask him,
　　do you want to take
　　one more leaf
　　of my scented geranium
　　and see what will happen
　　if you keep trying to scribble
　　those meaningless
　　words
　　with the tip
　　of your filthy, soil-stained
　　fingernail?

The poet-boy, poet-man,
　　almost grown and still composing sad verses
　　he says nothing at first,
　　then finally,
　　with a sigh,
　　the proper answer:
　　No.

Already he begins to swell like a corpse,
   disgusting,
   a horror
So I command the priest
Bathe him, I say
Apply ointments,
   take care of this poor child
Don't you know how to be merciful
and kind?

JUAN

~ ~ ~ ~ ~

For three days I am nowhere
    I do not exist
For three more days I am somewhere
    in pain

At night my mother sneaks in and helps me learn
    how to walk on wounded legs
She tells me she has enough money
    to purchase my freedom

I remind her that our first owner already set me free

She cannot think of an answer,
    we both know it's true
    I'm already free
    in this land of dreams and legends
    island
    of fantasies
    where I almost
    exist

JUAN

~ ~ ~ ~ ~

I weep, I work, I wait,
   and then once again
   I'm accused

This time it's one tiny game hen
   that's missing
I am innocent
   but who will believe me?
So I tell the same truth
   over and over
   If I were brave enough to steal
   I would take myself
   and some books,
      not a bird!

THE OVERSEER

This time I tie him with rope and make him run
    in front of my horse,
    in front of two hungry, obedient dogs,
    in front of the hooves
    and the claws
    and the fangs
    and my whip.

Watch him fall!
    Now I speak to the dogs;
    watch them turn
    into wolves.

See how the teeth
    enter his cheek
    sinking in
    all the way
    to his molars.
    There are fangs in his legs too,
    look at the left one.
    What a shame
    if he is hurt so badly
    that he will never
    be able to walk.

I grab the rope,
I yank it to save him
   proud of my compassion
   and at the same time furious with him
   for dislocating his arm
   at the end of my rope.

Why does everything with him
   always have to be
   so complicated?

JUAN

~ ~ ~ ~ ~

The worst is over, I imagine,
   I hope
   now I'm walking again,
   on these bleeding legs
   walking and walking
   until we finally reach the sugar mill
   where I will rest
   in the stocks
   while receiving my twenty-five
   lashes

Seven officials gather around me,
   demanding answers
   do they imagine that the overseer
   will dare to let me go
   if I tell the truth again and again?
   or do they imagine that I will be released
   if I try a few lies
   and claim that I took the missing game hen:
   I ate it
   the meat was tender
   my belly is full?
   or what about this one:
   I took it to sell

so that I could buy a fancy hat
for courting the sweet, pretty girls?

I choose the hat,
and seven officials now want to see it
but there is no hat
only the one
I imagined
so I say I bought shoes,
but I have no shoes
the questions and answers go on and on
I tell a thousand and one lies
trying to save myself
from the torment

JUAN

~ ~ ~ ~ ~

Seven thousand stories for the seven officials,
    then eight thousand,
    nine thousand,
    ten
    but none of my fantasies are false enough
    to rescue me
    from these people who keep shouting:

TELL THE TRUTH!

So instead of speaking I begin to dream
    of the various saints' opinions
    on the location of paradise
    east, west, north, south,
    up, always up,
    never down

I dream of my mother and brothers
    free in their small bell-shaped hut
    thatched with singing, wind-rustled,
    dry leaves of palm
    they are free
    so am I
    more or less

I dream of streets, narrow and shady
    to protect the people walking on them
    from sun
    cobblestone streets that follow the directions
    of the four invisible winds
    I see the winds flying
    escaping from
    town

JUAN

~ ~ ~ ~ ~

The nine nights of terror and dreaming are over
  because finally a brave muleteer has admitted
  that he saw the steward eating a game hen

So now I am free, in a sense
  free to work, and my jobs are these:
  forgetting to dream while I drive the oxen,
  burn the cane,
  press the juice of sweet sugar
  into a syrup
  of courage

Forgetting the truth while I carry the sugar
  walking even though my leg is damaged
  and I cannot
  walk

Forgetting anger while I place cones of sugarloaf
  in a shed

Forgetting,
  the hardest form of work
  and then suddenly, as swift as lightning
  disaster again

here it comes
a piece of the roof of the shed
as it falls,
I leap to escape death
even though I can't forget that death
was the thing I wished for every second
of those long, strange nine days

The slave standing beside me
stacking cones of sugarloaf in the shed by my side
has been crushed.

His name is Andrés.
He was born on this island,
a native
like me.
His name was Andrés.

MARÍA DEL PILAR

~ ~ ~ ~

Twice his freedom has been promised
 this time I paid,
 yet the act is denied
 I've been tricked,
 I'm a fool
 but after seeing
 the crushed skull
 and scraped skin
 and broken eyes
 of Andrés
 I knew I was right
 to try

Don Nicolás

~ ~ ~ ~ ~

My friend is sick in his spirit,
   his wounded soul
   his sorrowful heart
His brothers have spoken to me
   they beg me each day,
   please seek mercy
Don't be like your mother

So I take him back into the house
   where his only job is forgetting
   still, he will not eat
   or play with the children who call to him,
   begging for silly verses and fables
   and tales of imaginary
   heroes

All he does is weep while he works
   polishing his mind to clean it,
   trying to forget
   while he polishes the smooth wood
   of my mother's carved mahogany furniture

Now he has a hat and shoes,
   the ones I've given him

a hat and shoes just like
the ones he invented

I must have dreamed them out loud, he says
    my voice
    made them real

JUAN

~ ~ ~ ~

Can it be, is this true, O merciful Lord,
   did you actually hear my prayers and the begging
   of my brothers?

Suddenly I belong
   to Don Nicolás
   instead of his mother
   and he says I am his son
   not his slave
   even though
   we are the same age
   more or less

Miracles amaze me
watch how he pays me
   with coins
watch how he lets me buy cures
   for my fever, my cough
   a brew of cactus fruit and poppies
   orange blossoms, poplar leaves, milk and honey
   then dried beef mixed
   with chocolate
   for strengthening
   the lungs

DON NICOLÁS

He mends my clothes
   cleans my shoes
   tidies my room
   arranges my day
   my surroundings
   my desk

His affection for me
   knows no bounds
   and I know
   that it's only because
   he peeks
   at my books

JUAN

~ ~ ~ ~ ~

Almost free
    more or less
    just imagine:
    I am not allowed
    to go out alone
    or step into the kitchen
    where maids and cooks
    speak of indecent things
    but in all other ways I am free
    more or less

I tidy his chair, his desk, his books
    I give him a haven
    where he can study

I long to write
    so I use my new coins
    to buy quills and fine paper
    for tracing his words

Secretly I practice
    penmanship
    syllables
    symbols

letters that scatter
strange, wondrous meanings
across the wide world

I even copy the titles of paintings
until I am caught
then I pull out some sewing
and begin
to mend

At night when everyone else is asleep
I take a stub of candle
and copy the intricate verses of poets
whose long noble names are enclosed
in thick books

I write and rewrite and recite
every dream
along with a few
simple rhymes
of my own

DON NICOLÁS

~~~~~

I am ready
   to be married
   to Doña Teresa de Herrera

So I give Juan the tailor
   doubloons of gold
   each time he carries
   one of my secretive messages
   of love

María del Pilar

~ ~ ~ ~ ~

Suddenly my dear son is able to send
    so much money
    but is he free?
They've moved him to Guanajay where he sews
    for the bride of his master
They say God has given my son a strange gift
    not of verse but of hands
    the ability to stitch silken cloth
    and to heal
    wounded flesh

Suddenly he is famous
    for curing
    the ill

Counts and Countesses
    Dukes and Duchesses
    everyone sends for him
    whenever pain and fear
    are suffered

JUAN

~ ~ ~ ~ ~

Agony either makes a person want more pain
    for others
    or none at all
    for anyone
    anywhere
    any time

So I've learned to give baths
    of warm herbs and roots
    my vigils at bedsides
    are faithful
    I pray

And even though no one knows that I've learned
    how to write
    I do it
    I write
    every word
    that is moaned
    by my impatient
    patients
    as they wait
    to be healed

I keep a written record of the spitting and snoring
   the soundness of sleep
   and all the other things
   that should not be mentioned
   except in the presence
   of doctors
   and God

They come in the morning
   the doctors who praise my attention to details
   no matter how foul-scented, tragic, or hideous

I am famous
   but is fame
   a blessing
   or curse?

LA MARQUESA DE PRADO AMENO

He is famous
   and best of all
   he is mine.

I don't care how absurdly
   my son and his bride
   try to argue.

I have sent
   for the boy wizard
   the healer
   the mysterious wordsmith
   the slave
   he is mine.

Juan

~ ~ ~ ~ ~

I try everything I can think of
    begging
    pleading
    even a formal request to the magistrate
    written documents
    petitioning my transfer
    to a new master

She warns me to stop trying to talk
    to the priest and the courts

Have I ever harmed you? she asks
    in front of witnesses,
    so I'll know
    what I'm expected to say
    and to do

How dare you remember your mother, she says
    I am your mother
    this is your home

So once again I pretend
    that love and nature
    and logic

have all been replaced
by this nightmare
a vision
strange life
lost in dreams

JUAN

~~ ~~ ~~ ~~ ~~

One morning a rooster comes into the house
   and sings in my ear
   strange life

One day a free man insults my mother
   I fight
   unafraid of the lashes
   the pain

Day after day I hear conch shells blown
   as trumpets
   calling the field slaves to work before dawn
   grabbing their machetes for chopping the cane
   long sharp blades, so useless
   against guns

One day I run from the garden
   I hide
   in a swamp
   on the road
   to a castle
   strange feeling
   this courage
   this hope

JUAN

~ ~ ~ ~ ~

I walk to the castle and tell my story, asking for help
The Count of Jibacoa swears he will protect me
Soon those who know me,
    poets, scholars, doctors, priests
    step forth to defend me
    but a deputy comes

I am tied, draped in burlap
    they take my shoes, shave my head
    drag me back to the fields where I work
    side by side
    with these men who are marked
    by the shapes of their tribes
    carvings of stars, suns, and moons on dark cheeks
    teeth filed to points
    like the fangs of the lions they killed
    when they were warriors
    before the ships came and bought them
    from Arab slave traders who bought them
    from their own kings
    or the enemies
    who'd captured them
    in battle
    strange world

JUAN

~~ ~~ ~~ ~~ ~~

At night there are shooting stars, fireflies,
    wide-awake dreams
    I think of all the stories kitchen girls told me
    when I was little
    about mermaids dancing on waves
    trolls in the rivers
    tiny wishing wells
    GIANT WISHES
and I think of my mother reciting the songs
    of King David
    the one about a heart overflowing
    with a beautiful thought
    the one about a tongue like the pen
    of a skillful poet

I think of daily life
    stories of slaves who somehow ran away
    to secret forests
    hiding
    like pirates
    in villages
    surrounded
    by the magic
    of songs

La Marquesa de Prado Ameno

~ ~ ~ ~ ~

This time his punishment for running away is only
  nine days.

Then I fetch him and give him fine clothing
  again.

Then I take him to town in the coach
  like a prince
  more or less
  sitting beside the coachman
  practically
  a seat of honor.

Now we will see
  if he will be
  at least a little bit grateful
  this time
  at least a tiny bit grateful
  to me!

JUAN

~ ~ ~ ~ ~

Here I am in the house again
  hiding behind doors,
  reading books,
  all the poetry of San Juan de la Cruz
  poet-saint, prisoner, exile
  tortured, tormented, disbelieved, persecuted
  yet somehow the words,
  a strange fountain of hope:
  Apártalos, amado, que voy de vuelo . . .
  Look away, beloved, I'm going to fly . . .

and these words:
  A las aves ligeras,
  leones, ciervos, gamos saltadores,
  montes, valles, riberos,
  aguas, aires, ardores,
  y miedos de las noches veladores . . .
  O birds on easy wings,
  lions, stags, leaping fallow deer,
  mountains, valleys, shores,
  waters, winds, passions,
  and terror in the watchful nights . . .

and these words, strangest of all
   strangely easy to understand:
   Saber no sabiendo . . .
   To know without knowing . . .

To know without knowing
   a life filled with dreams
   heaven unseen
   strange faith, strangely real
   strangely mysterious fountain of words
   source of hope

So I let my mind fly
   free thoughts lifting, unseen
   up, up, up to the inviting
   unknown

JUAN

~ ~ ~ ~ ~

Out in the night
    slaves are dancing and drumming and singing.
    I smile
    then I cry
    in this house
    always hiding
    like a child
    behind doors
    book in hand.

JUAN

~ ~ ~ ~ ~

One day an artist comes to the house
   to paint flowers
   on an old glass display case
   he asks me to help
   and I do
   with delight
   unafraid to be caught shading roses
   with the magic
   of a brush

When he is finished he gives me a doubloon
   unaware that slaves are gambling out in the sheds
   I accept

Soon she comes, so ferocious, such strange hands,
   a wild search
   soon she finds the doubloon,
   sorrowful payment
   for roses
   fragrant flowers
   stench of doom

La Marquesa de Prado Ameno

～ ～ ～ ～ ～

How strangely he seems to have taken
    my sanity
    as if he were the master
    and I the slave
All my thoughts are of punishment
    but after nine days
    or ten
    eleven at most
    he comes back
    because I bring him,
    I fetch him,
    I almost apologize
    more or less
    as if I have allowed him to become
    the only person that matters
    in this, my strange life

He is in the fields
    being punished
    when the news comes
    about his mother
    so unexpected
    such a shock

So I send for him and tell him the sad news
    then I give him three whole coins
    for the priest
    to say a mass
    for her soul

JUAN

~ ~ ~ ~

How can I believe this?
    No, of course not,
    such a thing is not possible.
My mother gone
    nothing left
    but this old empty box
    in my hands
    the inheritance she left for me
    empty space
    enclosed
    by four small
    wooden walls.

So I find the secret compartment
    and inside I discover three bracelets of gold
    two rosaries, a crucifix
    a few dirty trinkets of coral
    and some paper:
        official documents proving
        that La Marquesa owed her money
        more than enough to purchase
        my freedom
        even though it has already been paid for
        and ignored.

Who could have guessed?
    That my mother owned a horse, then a colt,
    then more
    all of them sold to my owner
    in an effort to save enough wealth
    for me to purchase official documents proving
    that I own
    myself.

La Marquesa de Prado Ameno

~ ~ ~ ~ ~

How dare he ask to keep her things
    and collect her debts
    as if a mere slave could expect to receive
    an inheritance!

I tell him I am the heir of my slaves
    I say all you have belongs
    to me!

Then I add:
    If you speak of her money to me again
    you will never see
    moonlight or sunlight or stars!

Now go
    I command you
    this is my house
    see how it is filled with fine
    mahogany furniture
    from the forests
    of this lovely island?

Go, polish the wood,
    enjoy your freedom

to move through this house,
cleaning fine furniture
instead of rotting
in a dark, airless room
with dead bodies!

JUAN

~ ~ ~ ~ ~

I long for wings
   to fly away

The gold is my mother's
   a gift of love

I take her bracelets
   to the church

I sell them
   to buy candles

Airy flames
   a gift of love

For my mother's
   spirit

My prayers
   a fragrance

of words
   flying to God

DON NICOLÁS

~~~~~

What was he thinking,
   defying my mother?
   what did he expect?
   taking the gold bracelets
   selling them
   burning those candles
   all the gold bracelets vanishing
   strange alchemy
   worked in reverse
   changing jewelry
   to flames
   rising from candles
   flight of air
   life of dreams
   melting wax

JUAN

~~ ~~ ~~ ~~ ~~

Prison, of course,
    no matter that the bracelets
    should have been
    mine

A kind man comes
    and sets me free
    he shares his food
    and lets me sleep
    in the stable
    with horses,
    dreaming
    of wild manes
    and flying hooves

Soon La Marquesa comes to visit
    and the kind man has to put me
    in chains
Pretend, he whispers,
    pretend you have suffered the whip
    and the work
    and the weeping
    she expects

When nine days have passed
  she brings me a new set of elegant clothes

How weary I am of being rescued
  by my tormentor!

La Marquesa de Prado Ameno

~ ~ ~ ~ ~

I tell him to throw himself at my feet
I command him to beg my forgiveness
I order him to sit at my table and eat

His mouth never opens
   he won't speak, won't swallow

I'll send you fishing, I promise
   we'll go to the circus, together
   we'll see the funny clowns and the flying acrobats!

Still nothing, no verses, no words from the child
   or is he a man now?

Look, I'll let you study,
   you'll ride through the hills with my sons,
   you can gallop,
   how free and how fine
   you will feel!

His silence is torment.
   How dare he refuse
   to meet my eyes, smile, eat my food,
   give me thanks!

Don Nicolás

~ ~ ~ ~

Ah, Mother, my mother, how oddly she speaks,
    making him stand behind her
    while she plays those wild games
    of cards
    then giving him
    every coin
    she has won
    each and every coin
    without even counting
    her winnings

Can't she see, doesn't she hear
    his silent protests, feel the sharp edges
    of that look
    in his knifelike,
    wounded eyes?

All he wanted was candles
    to burn
    in the church,
    candles for God
    not this pile
    of gold
    won by gambling

Juan

~ ~ ~ ~ ~

I feel like a homing pigeon
   longing for my dovecote
   Havana is in my heart
   city of poets
   city of freedom
   streets of words
   alleys of wonder
   busy marketplace
   of ideas
   written and spoken
   shared and daydreamed
   embraced or rejected
   replaced or loaded
   onto the wings
   carried home

JUAN

~ ~ ~ ~ ~

La Marquesa seems to be noticing
   for the first time
   that I know how to sew my own clothes
   cook fancy pastries
   teach children their letters
   help them play with scraps of paper
   folding the treasure
   of discarded wrappers and letters to make
   flowers, seashells, pineapples, coins
   each folded papery shape so nearly weightless
   that it can be carried aloft
   by the gentlest suggestion
   of wind

Juan

~ ~ ~ ~ ~

Poets, painters, doctors, actors,
    singers, sculptors, playwrights,
    lawyers, gentlemen,
    scoundrels, noblemen,
    artisans,
    all are invited; they come, eat, play card games,
    sit at her table, laugh and gossip,
    recite monologues,
    whisper secrets,
    hand me books
    when no one is looking,
    smuggled verses
    for me to read
    like a frightened child
    hidden
    in the silence
    of that dim space
    behind
    every open
    door

Later I copy the smuggled poems
    then set them aside
    and write verses of my own

and whenever La Marquesa is not angry
I try to treat her as kindly
as she imagines her words,
her gifts and actions toward me,
have always deserved

Strange possession
these other secret words, gifts, and actions
the ones I create
in my mind
for myself

JUAN

~ ~ ~ ~ ~

I think of my mother's Psalms of faith
　　a single prayer
　　and even the excited words of kitchen girls
　　believing so many different things
　　all at the same time
　　saints, mermaids,
　　Lord of Lords,
　　river trolls,
　　one God, many demons,
　　one love, many hatreds,
　　on and on
　　always decided
　　and undecided
　　at the same time
　　always heated
　　by fiery new
　　possibilities

My verses are icy
　　no warmth
　　no love

Yet somehow I sell them
　　strangers come

from far away
to buy each silly
thing I say
empty rhymes
for troubled times
empty heart
meaningless art

JUAN

~ ~ ~ ~ ~

Havana is only twelve leagues away
    from this palace of wishes
    where I am the weaver of fairy tales,
    turning straw into gold with my words
    gold for strangers
    straw for myself.

I feel like a carpenter carving puppets
    of rhyme
    wooden words
    not true verses
    not alive
    like true rhymes
    of hope
    and love.

Juan

~ ~ ~ ~

There is a girl who lives close by
   angelic Muse
   I give her flowers
   the ones called marvel-of-Peru

She gives me candy, her smile, fresh fruit
   and one kiss
   the kind that sets
   enchanted frog-princes
   free

I tell her the truth
   I tell her I am free

No more stony palace of wishes
   for me

My verses are born now
   alive
   so new

No need to write them on flimsy paper
   how could my heart ever forget
   anything so true?

JUAN

~ ~ ~ ~ ~

Love is not enough
  to end the strange reality
  of a strangely lived
  life

This is how it happens:
  I go to the stream to bathe
  as always
  far from the country house
  far out of view

La Marquesa sends for me and says,
  who gave you permission
  to bathe?

No one, I answer
Then why? she demands
To be clean, I say calmly

The blow is a fierce one, the fist of a beast
  smashing my nose, crushing the bone
  opening two spurting fountains
  of blood

When her noblewoman's delicate fist has completed
    its secretive labor,
    destruction,
    then she calls for men
    to take my shoes, shave my head,
    make me carry a barrel of water
    up a hill
    over and over; I try but I fall
    until both the barrel and I end up
    splashing
    spilling
    rolling
    spitting blood
    into the stream

JUAN

~ ~ ~ ~ ~

The night is dark
   no moon
   curtains of rain
   heavy gloom

I've never done it before but now
   I lift
   a saddle
   onto
   a horse

On my knees
   in the mud
   I pray
   Lord I trust
   this strange life
   of mine
   to the unknown

I put on a hat
   mount the horse
   ride away

The last thing I hear
    is a voice
    God be with you
    hurry, hurry,
    don't delay!

At first I think I must be imagining
    the voice
Then I realize I'd imagined
    I was hidden by darkness, gloom, and rain

Now I know
    now I see
    through the gloom
    many watch me
    many slaves
    and many free
    dark and light and in-between
    all are praying
    many voices
    many languages
    from Africa
    and all the various
    dialects of Spain
    many voices
    praying for me

So many voices
    wishing me well, crying out
    God be with you
    hurry, hurry
    don't delay!

So many voices, joined as one
    so many eyes in the gloom
    seeing through darkness
    watching me, singing out hopefully
    as I escape!

ACKNOWLEDGMENTS

~ ~ ~ ~ ~

I am deeply grateful to Juan Francisco Manzano for having written poems that haunt me.

I will always be thankful to a generous God, my patient family, and the First Amendment to the U.S. Constitution, for giving me the peace of mind and the physical and intellectual freedom to write about Manzano's life and his poetry.

I wish to express profound respect and warm gratitude to Reka Simonsen for her gentle yet perceptive editorial suggestions, and for believing in this manuscript from the start, and giving it a home.

A hug to Robin Tordini for pulling my manuscript out of the "slush pile" and placing it in Reka's hands.

Admiration and gratitude to Sean Qualls for his artistic genius.

Many thanks to the entire friendly staff at Henry Holt for their treasured support and assistance, especially the copy editor, Deirdre Hare Jacobson, and the designer, Patrick Collins.

I am indebted to the following resources for factual information:

1. *Biblioteca Básica de Autores Cubanos.* "Juan Francisco

Manzano." Obras. Instituto Cubano Del Libro, Clasificación Biblioteca Nacional: 928.60.

2. *Autobiography of a Slave/Autobiografía de un Esclavo, a Bilingual Edition.* By Juan Francisco Manzano. Introduction and modernized Spanish version by Ivan A. Schulman. Translated by Evelyn Picon Garfield. Detroit: Wayne State University Press, 1996.

3. *The Life and Poems of a Cuban Slave: Juan Francisco Manzano.* Edited by Edward J. Mullen. North Haven, Conn.: Archon Books, 1981.

Historical Note

~ ~ ~ ~ ~

The life of Juan Francisco Manzano haunted me for years before I finally realized that to do justice to the Poet Slave's story, I needed to write it in verse.

Juan often said that he hoped to write a novel about his life. He never had the chance. In fact, strict censorship by the colonial Spanish government prevented all Cuban poets and novelists from writing verses or stories about slavery.

The life story of Juan Francisco Manzano is known only because some of his autobiographical notes were smuggled to England, where they were published by abolitionists who hoped to raise support for their cause.

Unfortunately, the second half of Juan's brief autobiography was lost in transport. As a result, little is known about the years after his courageous escape on horseback. We do know that he lived as a fugitive in Havana for many years, attending poetry readings and publishing books of his own poems while still officially a runaway slave. He married Delia, a mixed-race woman he called his Muse, for her beauty and her ability to play the piano inspired him to write verse. Her parents objected to the marriage because Juan's skin was darker than hers and because he was still technically a slave.

Eventually, Juan used his own income, along with collections taken up by friends and colleagues, to purchase his freedom, even though it had already been granted by his first owner and paid for by his mother.

Admired both as a poet and an honest man, Juan Francisco Manzano also gained fame as a confectioner, using the candymaking skills he'd learned while enslaved. At various times he worked as a tailor, painter, and cook, all trades he'd learned before attaining his freedom.

Then, in 1842, a year that became known as Cuba's Año del Cuero (Year of the Lash), false rumors of a slave rebellion resulted in the arrest of hundreds of people of all races, including many slaves and many poets.

Poetry has always been a powerful force in Latin American history, and poets have been regarded by dozens of governments, including the Spanish colonial one, as dangerous. This perception has arisen because so many poets choose to describe simple truths that affect both the emotions and the social awareness of readers and listeners.

During Juan Francisco Manzano's lifetime, Cubans gathered in homes to hear him read his poems. Those who knew how to read bought his books. People who could not read listened, memorized, and recited his words of hope. Poetry was as much a part of daily life then as television is now.

Because of his ability to influence people, Juan was arrested on charges of trying to stir up a slave rebellion. He had written nothing treasonous, and no actual rebellion had occurred, but Juan and many other Cuban poets were victims of a general atmosphere of fear and suspicion created by the chaos following a series of disastrous hurricanes. With mansions in ruins and crops destroyed, wealthy planters imagined that slaves would take advantage of the confusion to kill them and take over farms. Rumors based on these fears led to the mass execution of innocent poets who had done nothing more than express their feelings in verse.

Juan Francisco Manzano was one of the fortunate few who survived. He was released from prison in 1845. By then, it was clear that there had never been any plans for a rebellion. This tragic period in Cuban history is referred to as the Escalera Conspiracy, named for the ladders where slaves and poets were tied while being whipped.

Even though he survived, Juan was undoubtedly shocked, saddened, and terrified by his year in prison. His brilliant voice was silenced. If he wrote any more verses during the remaining nine years of his life, he must have kept them secret, because none were published. Those years of silence are a powerful testimony to the horror of censorship. Nevertheless, the poetic genius and dramatic life story of Juan Francisco Manzano, the Poet Slave of Cuba, provide us with an even more powerful and inspiring testimony to the ultimate triumph of freedom.

THE POETRY OF JUAN FRANCISCO MANZANO

~ ~ ~ ~ ~

The following are a few examples of Juan Francisco Manzano's capacity for hope. His verses show how he was determined to find beauty and goodness in a world filled with hideous cruelty.

Each excerpt is presented first in the original, rhymed, nineteenth-century Spanish, and then in my own modernized translation. I have attempted to retain the mood and meaning instead of the meter and rhyme.

1. An excerpt from "Dreams" ("Ilusiones"):

Sí, yo la ví una noche . . . ¡Cuán hermosa
Me pareció esta vez entre otras bellas!
Mas de un afecto tierno que hasta entonces
Ignoraba me fue—sentí en el alma
La dulce agitación del seno
El plácido latir, y el grato anhelo
De vivir para amar y ser dichoso . . .

~ ~ ~

Yes, I saw her one night . . . How beautiful
She seemed to me this time, as always!
And from a tender affection up until then
Ignored—I felt in my soul
The sweet agitation of breath

The quiet pulse, and the pleasant desire
To live for love and to be happy . . .

2. An excerpt from "My Thirty Years" ("Mis treinta
   años") shows how even moments of discouragement
   can be a source of awareness of one's own strength:

Cuando miro el espacio que he corrido
desde la cuna hasta el presente día,
tiemblo y saludo a la fortuna mía
más de terror que de atención movido.

Sorpréndeme la lucha que he podido
sostener contra suerte tan impía,
si tal llamarse puede la porfía
de mi infelice ser al mal nacido . . .

~ ~ ~

When I look back at the distance I've run
from the cradle to this present day,
I tremble and greet my fortune
more with terror than polite attention.

I marvel at the struggle I've managed
to endure against such drastic luck,
if it can even be called luck, this persistent
unhappiness of one so poorly born . . .

3. An excerpt from "The Firefly Hunter" ("La cocuyera") describes the Cuban tradition of capturing fireflies and wearing them as living hair ornaments, or keeping them in cages used as lanterns. This poem makes us wonder about the true nature of inner freedom, represented by the firefly's flashing light, sometimes visible and sometimes hidden:

Un incauto cocuyo
Revolaba brillando
Ya del prado a la selva.
Ya de la selva al prado.
Libre cual mariposa
Hendiendo el aire vago,
Liba en virgenes flores
Jugos almibarados
Ora esplende, ora oculta
Del fósforo inflamado
La luz a que no cabe
Color acomodado.
¡Cómo vuela invisible!
Lucero es ya bien claro:
Si puesto se oscurece,
Presto ilumina el campo. . . .

~ ~ ~

A careless firefly
circled, flickering
from the meadows to the forest.

Then from the forest to the meadow.
As free as a butterfly
wandering through the air,
sipping the juicy nectar
of fresh flowers
sometimes splendid,
sometimes hidden
the glowing flame
of a light that does not end
in a certain color.
Invisible, it flies!
The morning star is bright:
but when it sets
there is darkness,
and when it rises the land
is illuminated. . . .